THIS HOUSE BUYING HELPER BELONGS TO:

ADDRESS *Information*

CURRENT ADDRESS:

ESTATE AGENT:

NAME:
AGENCY:
PHONE:
EMAIL:

CLOSING DATE:

DATE:

CURRENT ADDRESS:

ESTATE AGENT:

NAME:
AGENCY:
PHONE:
EMAIL:

CLOSING DATE:

DATE:

NOTES & REMINDERS

IMPORTANT *Contacts*

CLOSING ATTORNEY

NAME:

ADDRESS:

EMAIL:

PHONE:

MORTGAGE BROKER / COMPANY

NAME:

ADDRESS:

EMAIL:

PHONE:

MOVING COMPANY

NAME:

ADDRESS:

EMAIL:

PHONE:

HOME APPRAISER

NAME:

ADDRESS:

EMAIL:

PHONE:

NOTES & REMINDERS

IMPORTANT *dates & appointments*

MONTH						

NOTES & REMINDERS

MONEY
things

BUDGET *breakdown*

Financial commitments	Frequency	Amount
Rent		
Car loan repayments		
Credit card		
Other loan repayments		
Child support payments		
Donations/charity		
Pocket money		
Other		
Total		

Home & utilities		
Contents insurance		
New furniture/appliances		
Electricity		
Gas		
Water		
Internet		
Phone		
Subscriptions (Foxtel, Netflix)		
Other		
Total		

Education		
School fees		
Uni/TAFE		
Childcare/Pre-school		
School uniforms		
Sport, music, dance etc.		
Excursions		
Other		
Total		

Health		
Private health insurance		
Life insurance		
Doctors		
Dentists		
Medicines/Pharmacy		
Eyecare/Glasses		
Vet		
Other		
Total		

Transport	Frequency	Amount
Car insurance		
Car maintenance		
Car rego/licence		
Petrol		
Road tolls/parking		
Public transport		
Other		
Total		

Shopping		
Supermarket		
Baby products		
Clothing/shoes		
Cosmetics/toiletries		
Hairdresser		
Other		
Total		

Eating out		
Restaurants		
Takeaway		
Bought lunches		
Snacks		
Coffee		
Other		
Total		

Entertainment		
Bars/clubs		
Other alcohol		
Gym/sport memberships		
Cigarettes		
Movies/music		
Hobbies		
Newspaper/magazines		
Celebrations		
Other		
Total		

Total		

Now you know what you spend compared to how much you earn.

HOW MUCH CAN YOU SAVE TOWARD A HOUSE DEPOSIT IN A YEAR?

ARE THERE PLACES YOU COULD CUT BACK ON YOUR SPENDING?

ARE THERE OTHER WAYS YOU COULD INCREASE YOUR INCOME?

IN _____ I WILL SAVE:
months / years

FINANCIAL *plan*

| TOTAL SAVINGS GOAL: | _____ |

SLOW AND STEADY SAVING OVER TIME CAN BE MUCH LESS PAINFUL TO DO, AS YOU DON'T NEED TO MAKE SUCH BIG SACRIFICES TO REACH YOUR GOALS. HERE ARE SOME TECHNIQUES YOU MIGHT LIKE TO TRY.

52 WEEK MONEY SAVING Challenge

☑	WEEK	AMOUNT	BALANCE	☑	WEEK	AMOUNT	BALANCE
	1	$1	$1		27	$27	$378
	2	$2	$3		28	$28	$406
	3	$3	$6		29	$29	$435
	4	$4	$10		30	$30	$465
	5	$5	$15		31	$31	$496
	6	$6	$21		32	$32	$528
	7	$7	$28		33	$33	$561
	8	$8	$36		34	$34	$595
	9	$9	$45		35	$35	$630
	10	$10	$55		36	$36	$666
	11	$11	$66		37	$37	$703
	12	$12	$78		38	$38	$741
	13	$13	$91		39	$39	$780
	14	$14	$105		40	$40	$820
	15	$15	$120		41	$41	$861
	16	$16	$136		42	$42	$903
	17	$17	$153		43	$43	$946
	18	$18	$171		44	$44	$990
	19	$19	$190		45	$45	$1035
	20	$20	$210		46	$46	$1081
	21	$21	$231		47	$47	$1128
	22	$22	$253		48	$48	$1176
	23	$23	$276		49	$49	$1225
	24	$24	$300		50	$50	$1275
	25	$25	$325		51	$51	$1326
	26	$26	$351		52	$52	$1378

KEEPING TRACK OF
the house fund

TOTAL _____

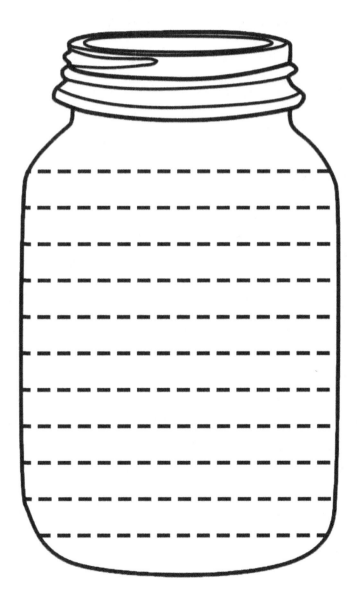

- December
- November
- October
- September
- August
- July
- June
- May
- April
- March
- February
- January

BILL Tracker

MONTH OF:

UTILITIES	BUDGET	SPENT
ELECTRIC	$	$
GAS	$	$
TRASH	$	$
INTERNET	$	$
PHONE	$	$
TOTAL	$	$

PERSONAL	BUDGET	SPENT
ENTERTAINMENT	$	$
CLOTHING	$	$
COSMETICS	$	$
LIFE INSURANCE	$	$
OTHER	$	$
TOTAL	$	$

HOME	BUDGET	SPENT
RENT/MORTGAGE	$	$
TAXES	$	$
INSURANCE	$	$
REPAIRS	$	$
TOTAL	$	$

TRANSPORTATION	BUDGET	SPENT
CAR PAYMENT	$	$
CAR INSURANCE	$	$
GAS	$	$
MAINTENANCE	$	$
TOTAL	$	$

FOOD	BUDGET	SPENT
GROCERIES	$	$
EATING OUT	$	$
TOTAL	$	$

MEDICAL	BUDGET	SPENT
DOCTOR BILLS	$	$
MEDICATION	$	$
TOTAL	$	$

GIVING	BUDGET	SPENT
TITHES	$	$
CHARITY	$	$
TOTAL	$	$

DEBTS	BUDGET	SPENT
CREDIT CARD	$	$
OTHER	$	$
TOTAL	$	$

INCOME

DATE	FROM WHERE?	AMT

CHECKING ACCOUNT

STARTING	GOAL	ENDING

SAVINGS ACCOUNT

STARTING	GOAL	ENDING

NOTES:

BILL *Tracker*

MONTH OF:

UTILITIES	BUDGET	SPENT
ELECTRIC	$	$
GAS	$	$
TRASH	$	$
INTERNET	$	$
PHONE	$	$
TOTAL	$	$

PERSONAL	BUDGET	SPENT
ENTERTAINMENT	$	$
CLOTHING	$	$
COSMETICS	$	$
LIFE INSURANCE	$	$
OTHER	$	$
TOTAL	$	$

HOME	BUDGET	SPENT
RENT/MORTGAGE	$	$
TAXES	$	$
INSURANCE	$	$
REPAIRS	$	$
TOTAL	$	$

TRANSPORTATION	BUDGET	SPENT
CAR PAYMENT	$	$
CAR INSURANCE	$	$
GAS	$	$
MAINTENANCE	$	$
TOTAL	$	$

FOOD	BUDGET	SPENT
GROCERIES	$	$
EATING OUT	$	$
TOTAL	$	$

MEDICAL	BUDGET	SPENT
DOCTOR BILLS	$	$
MEDICATION	$	$
TOTAL	$	$

GIVING	BUDGET	SPENT
TITHES	$	$
CHARITY	$	$
TOTAL	$	$

DEBTS	BUDGET	SPENT
CREDIT CARD	$	$
OTHER	$	$
TOTAL	$	$

INCOME

DATE	FROM WHERE?	AMT

CHECKING ACCOUNT

STARTING	GOAL	ENDING

SAVINGS ACCOUNT

STARTING	GOAL	ENDING

NOTES:

BILL Tracker

MONTH OF:

UTILITIES	BUDGET	SPENT
ELECTRIC	$	$
GAS	$	$
TRASH	$	$
INTERNET	$	$
PHONE	$	$
TOTAL	$	$

PERSONAL	BUDGET	SPENT
ENTERTAINMENT	$	$
CLOTHING	$	$
COSMETICS	$	$
LIFE INSURANCE	$	$
OTHER	$	$
TOTAL	$	$

HOME	BUDGET	SPENT
RENT/MORTGAGE	$	$
TAXES	$	$
INSURANCE	$	$
REPAIRS	$	$
TOTAL	$	$

TRANSPORTATION	BUDGET	SPENT
CAR PAYMENT	$	$
CAR INSURANCE	$	$
GAS	$	$
MAINTENANCE	$	$
TOTAL	$	$

FOOD	BUDGET	SPENT
GROCERIES	$	$
EATING OUT	$	$
TOTAL	$	$

MEDICAL	BUDGET	SPENT
DOCTOR BILLS	$	$
MEDICATION	$	$
TOTAL	$	$

GIVING	BUDGET	SPENT
TITHES	$	$
CHARITY	$	$
TOTAL	$	$

DEBTS	BUDGET	SPENT
CREDIT CARD	$	$
OTHER	$	$
TOTAL	$	$

INCOME

DATE	FROM WHERE?	AMT

CHECKING ACCOUNT

STARTING	GOAL	ENDING

SAVINGS ACCOUNT

STARTING	GOAL	ENDING

NOTES:

BILL *Tracker*

MONTH OF:

UTILITIES	BUDGET	SPENT
ELECTRIC	$	$
GAS	$	$
TRASH	$	$
INTERNET	$	$
PHONE	$	$
TOTAL	$	$

PERSONAL	BUDGET	SPENT
ENTERTAINMENT	$	$
CLOTHING	$	$
COSMETICS	$	$
LIFE INSURANCE	$	$
OTHER	$	$
TOTAL	$	$

HOME	BUDGET	SPENT
RENT/MORTGAGE	$	$
TAXES	$	$
INSURANCE	$	$
REPAIRS	$	$
TOTAL	$	$

TRANSPORTATION	BUDGET	SPENT
CAR PAYMENT	$	$
CAR INSURANCE	$	$
GAS	$	$
MAINTENANCE	$	$
TOTAL	$	$

FOOD	BUDGET	SPENT
GROCERIES	$	$
EATING OUT	$	$
TOTAL	$	$

MEDICAL	BUDGET	SPENT
DOCTOR BILLS	$	$
MEDICATION	$	$
TOTAL	$	$

GIVING	BUDGET	SPENT
TITHES	$	$
CHARITY	$	$
TOTAL	$	$

DEBTS	BUDGET	SPENT
CREDIT CARD	$	$
OTHER	$	$
TOTAL	$	$

INCOME

DATE	FROM WHERE?	AMT

CHECKING ACCOUNT

STARTING	GOAL	ENDING

SAVINGS ACCOUNT

STARTING	GOAL	ENDING

NOTES:

BILL Tracker

MONTH OF:

UTILITIES	BUDGET	SPENT
ELECTRIC	$	$
GAS	$	$
TRASH	$	$
INTERNET	$	$
PHONE	$	$
TOTAL	$	$

PERSONAL	BUDGET	SPENT
ENTERTAINMENT	$	$
CLOTHING	$	$
COSMETICS	$	$
LIFE INSURANCE	$	$
OTHER	$	$
TOTAL	$	$

HOME	BUDGET	SPENT
RENT/MORTGAGE	$	$
TAXES	$	$
INSURANCE	$	$
REPAIRS	$	$
TOTAL	$	$

TRANSPORTATION	BUDGET	SPENT
CAR PAYMENT	$	$
CAR INSURANCE	$	$
GAS	$	$
MAINTENANCE	$	$
TOTAL	$	$

FOOD	BUDGET	SPENT
GROCERIES	$	$
EATING OUT	$	$
TOTAL	$	$

MEDICAL	BUDGET	SPENT
DOCTOR BILLS	$	$
MEDICATION	$	$
TOTAL	$	$

GIVING	BUDGET	SPENT
TITHES	$	$
CHARITY	$	$
TOTAL	$	$

DEBTS	BUDGET	SPENT
CREDIT CARD	$	$
OTHER	$	$
TOTAL	$	$

INCOME		
DATE	FROM WHERE?	AMT

CHECKING ACCOUNT

STARTING	GOAL	ENDING

SAVINGS ACCOUNT

STARTING	GOAL	ENDING

NOTES:

BILL *Tracker*

MONTH OF:

UTILITIES	BUDGET	SPENT
ELECTRIC	$	$
GAS	$	$
TRASH	$	$
INTERNET	$	$
PHONE	$	$
TOTAL	$	$

PERSONAL	BUDGET	SPENT
ENTERTAINMENT	$	$
CLOTHING	$	$
COSMETICS	$	$
LIFE INSURANCE	$	$
OTHER	$	$
TOTAL	$	$

HOME	BUDGET	SPENT
RENT/MORTGAGE	$	$
TAXES	$	$
INSURANCE	$	$
REPAIRS	$	$
TOTAL	$	$

TRANSPORTATION	BUDGET	SPENT
CAR PAYMENT	$	$
CAR INSURANCE	$	$
GAS	$	$
MAINTENANCE	$	$
TOTAL	$	$

FOOD	BUDGET	SPENT
GROCERIES	$	$
EATING OUT	$	$
TOTAL	$	$

MEDICAL	BUDGET	SPENT
DOCTOR BILLS	$	$
MEDICATION	$	$
TOTAL	$	$

GIVING	BUDGET	SPENT
TITHES	$	$
CHARITY	$	$
TOTAL	$	$

DEBTS	BUDGET	SPENT
CREDIT CARD	$	$
OTHER	$	$
TOTAL	$	$

INCOME

DATE	FROM WHERE?	AMT

CHECKING ACCOUNT

STARTING	GOAL	ENDING

SAVINGS ACCOUNT

STARTING	GOAL	ENDING

NOTES:

BILL Tracker

MONTH OF:

UTILITIES	BUDGET	SPENT
ELECTRIC	$	$
GAS	$	$
TRASH	$	$
INTERNET	$	$
PHONE	$	$
TOTAL	$	$

PERSONAL	BUDGET	SPENT
ENTERTAINMENT	$	$
CLOTHING	$	$
COSMETICS	$	$
LIFE INSURANCE	$	$
OTHER	$	$
TOTAL	$	$

HOME	BUDGET	SPENT
RENT/MORTGAGE	$	$
TAXES	$	$
INSURANCE	$	$
REPAIRS	$	$
TOTAL	$	$

TRANSPORTATION	BUDGET	SPENT
CAR PAYMENT	$	$
CAR INSURANCE	$	$
GAS	$	$
MAINTENANCE	$	$
TOTAL	$	$

FOOD	BUDGET	SPENT
GROCERIES	$	$
EATING OUT	$	$
TOTAL	$	$

MEDICAL	BUDGET	SPENT
DOCTOR BILLS	$	$
MEDICATION	$	$
TOTAL	$	$

GIVING	BUDGET	SPENT
TITHES	$	$
CHARITY	$	$
TOTAL	$	$

DEBTS	BUDGET	SPENT
CREDIT CARD	$	$
OTHER	$	$
TOTAL	$	$

INCOME

DATE	FROM WHERE?	AMT

CHECKING ACCOUNT

STARTING	GOAL	ENDING

SAVINGS ACCOUNT

STARTING	GOAL	ENDING

NOTES:

BILL *Tracker*

MONTH OF:

UTILITIES	BUDGET	SPENT		PERSONAL	BUDGET	SPENT
ELECTRIC	$	$		ENTERTAINMENT	$	$
GAS	$	$		CLOTHING	$	$
TRASH	$	$		COSMETICS	$	$
INTERNET	$	$		LIFE INSURANCE	$	$
PHONE	$	$		OTHER	$	$
TOTAL	$	$		TOTAL	$	$

HOME	BUDGET	SPENT		TRANSPORTATION	BUDGET	SPENT
RENT/MORTGAGE	$	$		CAR PAYMENT	$	$
TAXES	$	$		CAR INSURANCE	$	$
INSURANCE	$	$		GAS	$	$
REPAIRS	$	$		MAINTENANCE	$	$
TOTAL	$	$		TOTAL	$	$

FOOD	BUDGET	SPENT		MEDICAL	BUDGET	SPENT
GROCERIES	$	$		DOCTOR BILLS	$	$
EATING OUT	$	$		MEDICATION	$	$
TOTAL	$	$		TOTAL	$	$

GIVING	BUDGET	SPENT		DEBTS	BUDGET	SPENT
TITHES	$	$		CREDIT CARD	$	$
CHARITY	$	$		OTHER	$	$
TOTAL	$	$		TOTAL	$	$

INCOME

DATE	FROM WHERE?	AMT

CHECKING ACCOUNT

STARTING	GOAL	ENDING

SAVINGS ACCOUNT

STARTING	GOAL	ENDING

NOTES:

BILL *Tracker*

MONTH OF:

UTILITIES	BUDGET	SPENT
ELECTRIC	$	$
GAS	$	$
TRASH	$	$
INTERNET	$	$
PHONE	$	$
TOTAL	$	$

PERSONAL	BUDGET	SPENT
ENTERTAINMENT	$	$
CLOTHING	$	$
COSMETICS	$	$
LIFE INSURANCE	$	$
OTHER	$	$
TOTAL	$	$

HOME	BUDGET	SPENT
RENT/MORTGAGE	$	$
TAXES	$	$
INSURANCE	$	$
REPAIRS	$	$
TOTAL	$	$

TRANSPORTATION	BUDGET	SPENT
CAR PAYMENT	$	$
CAR INSURANCE	$	$
GAS	$	$
MAINTENANCE	$	$
TOTAL	$	$

FOOD	BUDGET	SPENT
GROCERIES	$	$
EATING OUT	$	$
TOTAL	$	$

MEDICAL	BUDGET	SPENT
DOCTOR BILLS	$	$
MEDICATION	$	$
TOTAL	$	$

GIVING	BUDGET	SPENT
TITHES	$	$
CHARITY	$	$
TOTAL	$	$

DEBTS	BUDGET	SPENT
CREDIT CARD	$	$
OTHER	$	$
TOTAL	$	$

INCOME

DATE	FROM WHERE?	AMT

CHECKING ACCOUNT

STARTING	GOAL	ENDING

SAVINGS ACCOUNT

STARTING	GOAL	ENDING

NOTES:

BILL *Tracker*

MONTH OF:

UTILITIES	BUDGET	SPENT
ELECTRIC	$	$
GAS	$	$
TRASH	$	$
INTERNET	$	$
PHONE	$	$
TOTAL	$	$

PERSONAL	BUDGET	SPENT
ENTERTAINMENT	$	$
CLOTHING	$	$
COSMETICS	$	$
LIFE INSURANCE	$	$
OTHER	$	$
TOTAL	$	$

HOME	BUDGET	SPENT
RENT/MORTGAGE	$	$
TAXES	$	$
INSURANCE	$	$
REPAIRS	$	$
TOTAL	$	$

TRANSPORTATION	BUDGET	SPENT
CAR PAYMENT	$	$
CAR INSURANCE	$	$
GAS	$	$
MAINTENANCE	$	$
TOTAL	$	$

FOOD	BUDGET	SPENT
GROCERIES	$	$
EATING OUT	$	$
TOTAL	$	$

MEDICAL	BUDGET	SPENT
DOCTOR BILLS	$	$
MEDICATION	$	$
TOTAL	$	$

GIVING	BUDGET	SPENT
TITHES	$	$
CHARITY	$	$
TOTAL	$	$

DEBTS	BUDGET	SPENT
CREDIT CARD	$	$
OTHER	$	$
TOTAL	$	$

INCOME

DATE	FROM WHERE?	AMT

CHECKING ACCOUNT

STARTING	GOAL	ENDING

SAVINGS ACCOUNT

STARTING	GOAL	ENDING

NOTES:

BILL *Tracker*

MONTH OF:

UTILITIES	BUDGET	SPENT
ELECTRIC	$	$
GAS	$	$
TRASH	$	$
INTERNET	$	$
PHONE	$	$
TOTAL	$	$

PERSONAL	BUDGET	SPENT
ENTERTAINMENT	$	$
CLOTHING	$	$
COSMETICS	$	$
LIFE INSURANCE	$	$
OTHER	$	$
TOTAL	$	$

HOME	BUDGET	SPENT
RENT/MORTGAGE	$	$
TAXES	$	$
INSURANCE	$	$
REPAIRS	$	$
TOTAL	$	$

TRANSPORTATION	BUDGET	SPENT
CAR PAYMENT	$	$
CAR INSURANCE	$	$
GAS	$	$
MAINTENANCE	$	$
TOTAL	$	$

FOOD	BUDGET	SPENT
GROCERIES	$	$
EATING OUT	$	$
TOTAL	$	$

MEDICAL	BUDGET	SPENT
DOCTOR BILLS	$	$
MEDICATION	$	$
TOTAL	$	$

GIVING	BUDGET	SPENT
TITHES	$	$
CHARITY	$	$
TOTAL	$	$

DEBTS	BUDGET	SPENT
CREDIT CARD	$	$
OTHER	$	$
TOTAL	$	$

INCOME

DATE	FROM WHERE?	AMT

CHECKING ACCOUNT

STARTING	GOAL	ENDING

SAVINGS ACCOUNT

STARTING	GOAL	ENDING

NOTES:

BILL *Tracker*

MONTH OF:

UTILITIES	BUDGET	SPENT
ELECTRIC	$	$
GAS	$	$
TRASH	$	$
INTERNET	$	$
PHONE	$	$
TOTAL	$	$

PERSONAL	BUDGET	SPENT
ENTERTAINMENT	$	$
CLOTHING	$	$
COSMETICS	$	$
LIFE INSURANCE	$	$
OTHER	$	$
TOTAL	$	$

HOME	BUDGET	SPENT
RENT/MORTGAGE	$	$
TAXES	$	$
INSURANCE	$	$
REPAIRS	$	$
TOTAL	$	$

TRANSPORTATION	BUDGET	SPENT
CAR PAYMENT	$	$
CAR INSURANCE	$	$
GAS	$	$
MAINTENANCE	$	$
TOTAL	$	$

FOOD	BUDGET	SPENT
GROCERIES	$	$
EATING OUT	$	$
TOTAL	$	$

MEDICAL	BUDGET	SPENT
DOCTOR BILLS	$	$
MEDICATION	$	$
TOTAL	$	$

GIVING	BUDGET	SPENT
TITHES	$	$
CHARITY	$	$
TOTAL	$	$

DEBTS	BUDGET	SPENT
CREDIT CARD	$	$
OTHER	$	$
TOTAL	$	$

INCOME

DATE	FROM WHERE?	AMT

CHECKING ACCOUNT

STARTING	GOAL	ENDING

SAVINGS ACCOUNT

STARTING	GOAL	ENDING

NOTES:

BILL *Tracker*

MONTH OF:

UTILITIES	BUDGET	SPENT
ELECTRIC	$	$
GAS	$	$
TRASH	$	$
INTERNET	$	$
PHONE	$	$
TOTAL	$	$

PERSONAL	BUDGET	SPENT
ENTERTAINMENT	$	$
CLOTHING	$	$
COSMETICS	$	$
LIFE INSURANCE	$	$
OTHER	$	$
TOTAL	$	$

HOME	BUDGET	SPENT
RENT/MORTGAGE	$	$
TAXES	$	$
INSURANCE	$	$
REPAIRS	$	$
TOTAL	$	$

TRANSPORTATION	BUDGET	SPENT
CAR PAYMENT	$	$
CAR INSURANCE	$	$
GAS	$	$
MAINTENANCE	$	$
TOTAL	$	$

FOOD	BUDGET	SPENT
GROCERIES	$	$
EATING OUT	$	$
TOTAL	$	$

MEDICAL	BUDGET	SPENT
DOCTOR BILLS	$	$
MEDICATION	$	$
TOTAL	$	$

GIVING	BUDGET	SPENT
TITHES	$	$
CHARITY	$	$
TOTAL	$	$

DEBTS	BUDGET	SPENT
CREDIT CARD	$	$
OTHER	$	$
TOTAL	$	$

INCOME

DATE	FROM WHERE?	AMT

CHECKING ACCOUNT

STARTING	GOAL	ENDING

SAVINGS ACCOUNT

STARTING	GOAL	ENDING

NOTES:

FINDING THE
perfect home

PROPERTY INSPECTION *Checklist*

EXTERIOR CONDITION: GOOD   OK   BAD   **NOTES:**

- EXTERIOR OF PROPERTY
- FRONT DOOR
- PORCH/DECK/PATIO
- DRIVEWAY
- GARAGE DOORS
- OUTDOOR LIGHTING
- PAINT & TRIM
- WINDOWS
- WALKWAY

ROOF CONDITION: GOOD   OK   BAD   **NOTES:**

- CHIMNEY
- GUTTERS & DOWNSPOUTS
- SOFITS & FASCIA
- YEAR ROOF WAS REPLACED:

GARAGE CONDITION: GOOD   OK   BAD   **NOTES:**

- CEILING
- DOORS
- FLOORS & WALLS
- YEAR DOOR OPENERS WERE REPLACED:

YARD CONDITION: GOOD   OK   BAD   **NOTES:**

- DRAINAGE
- FENCES & GATES
- RETAINING WALL
- SPRINKLER SYSTEM

PROPERTY INSPECTION
Checklist

OTHER IMPORTANT AREAS: GOOD   OK   BAD   **NOTES:**

FOUNDATION

MASONRY VENEERS

EXTERIOR PAINT

STORM WINDOWS

PLUMBING

ELECTRICAL OUTLETS

FLOORING IN ROOMS

WOOD TRIM

FIREPLACE

KITCHEN CONDITION: GOOD   OK   BAD   **NOTES:**

WORKING EXHAUST FAN

NO LEAKS IN PIPES

APPLIANCES OPERATE

OTHER:

BATHROOM CONDITION: GOOD   OK   BAD   **NOTES:**

PROPER DRAINAGE

NO LEAKS IN PIPES

CAULKING IN GOOD SHAPE

TILES ARE SECURE

MISC: GOOD   OK   BAD   **NOTES:**

SMOKE & CARBON DETECTORS

STAIRWAY TREADS SOLID

STAIR HANDRAILS INSTALLED

OTHER:

OTHER:

OTHER:

HOUSE HUNTING *List*

ADDRESS	PRICE	NOTES

HOUSE HUNTING *List*

ADDRESS	PRICE	NOTES

HOUSE HUNTING *Checklist*

HOUSE SCORE:

PROPERTY ADDRESS

ASKING PRICE: PROPERTY TAXES:

LOT SIZE: PROPERTY SIZE:

FINISH: ☐ BRICK ☐ STUCCO   AGE OF PROPERTY:
         ☐ WOOD   ☐ SIDING

NEIGHBORHOOD

DISTANCE TO SCHOOLS: DISTANCE TO WORK:

PUBLIC TRANSPORTATION: MEDICAL:

RECREATION: SHOPPING:

ADDITIONAL INFO: NOTES:

HOUSE HUNTING

DETAILED HOUSE FEATURES:

OF BEDROOMS: # OF BATHROOMS:

BASEMENT: HEATING TYPE:

PROPERTY CHECKLIST:

				NOTES
POOL	☐	BONUS ROOM	☐	
GARAGE	☐	LAUNDRY CHUTE	☐	
FIREPLACE	☐	FENCED YARD	☐	
EN-SUITE	☐	APPLIANCES	☐	
OFFICE	☐	A/C	☐	
DECK	☐	HEAT PUMP	☐	

NOTES

PARKING ☐
CLOSETS ☐
STORAGE ☐

PROPERTY INSPECTION
Checklist

EXTERIOR CONDITION: GOOD OK BAD **NOTES:**

- EXTERIOR OF PROPERTY
- FRONT DOOR
- PORCH/DECK/PATIO
- DRIVEWAY
- GARAGE DOORS
- OUTDOOR LIGHTING
- PAINT & TRIM
- WINDOWS
- WALKWAY

ROOF CONDITION: GOOD OK BAD **NOTES:**

- CHIMNEY
- GUTTERS & DOWNSPOUTS
- SOFITS & FASCIA
- YEAR ROOF WAS REPLACED: _____

GARAGE CONDITION: GOOD OK BAD **NOTES:**

- CEILING
- DOORS
- FLOORS & WALLS
- YEAR DOOR OPENERS WERE REPLACED: _____

YARD CONDITION: GOOD OK BAD **NOTES:**

- DRAINAGE
- FENCES & GATES
- RETAINING WALL
- SPRINKLER SYSTEM

PROPERTY INSPECTION *Checklist*

OTHER IMPORTANT AREAS: GOOD OK BAD **NOTES:**

FOUNDATION

MASONRY VENEERS

EXTERIOR PAINT

STORM WINDOWS

PLUMBING

ELECTRICAL OUTLETS

FLOORING IN ROOMS

WOOD TRIM

FIREPLACE

KITCHEN CONDITION: GOOD OK BAD **NOTES:**

WORKING EXHAUST FAN

NO LEAKS IN PIPES

APPLIANCES OPERATE

OTHER:

BATHROOM CONDITION: GOOD OK BAD **NOTES:**

PROPER DRAINAGE

NO LEAKS IN PIPES

CAULKING IN GOOD SHAPE

TILES ARE SECURE

MISC: GOOD OK BAD **NOTES:**

SMOKE & CARBON DETECTORS

STAIRWAY TREADS SOLID

STAIR HANDRAILS INSTALLED

OTHER:

OTHER:

OTHER:

STICK FLOOR PLAN HERE
(if available)

HOUSE HUNTING Checklist

HOUSE SCORE:

PROPERTY ADDRESS

ASKING PRICE:

PROPERTY TAXES:

LOT SIZE:

PROPERTY SIZE:

FINISH:
- ☐ BRICK
- ☐ STUCCO
- ☐ WOOD
- ☐ SIDING

AGE OF PROPERTY:

NEIGHBORHOOD

DISTANCE TO SCHOOLS:

DISTANCE TO WORK:

PUBLIC TRANSPORTATION:

MEDICAL:

RECREATION:

SHOPPING:

ADDITIONAL INFO:

NOTES:

HOUSE HUNTING

DETAILED HOUSE FEATURES:

OF BEDROOMS: # OF BATHROOMS:

BASEMENT: HEATING TYPE:

PROPERTY CHECKLIST:

POOL	☐	BONUS ROOM	☐	NOTES
GARAGE	☐	LAUNDRY CHUTE	☐	
FIREPLACE	☐	FENCED YARD	☐	
EN-SUITE	☐	APPLIANCES	☐	
OFFICE	☐	A/C	☐	
DECK	☐	HEAT PUMP	☐	

PARKING	☐	NOTES
CLOSETS	☐	
STORAGE	☐	

PROPERTY INSPECTION *Checklist*

EXTERIOR CONDITION: GOOD OK BAD **NOTES:**

- EXTERIOR OF PROPERTY
- FRONT DOOR
- PORCH/DECK/PATIO
- DRIVEWAY
- GARAGE DOORS
- OUTDOOR LIGHTING
- PAINT & TRIM
- WINDOWS
- WALKWAY

ROOF CONDITION: GOOD OK BAD **NOTES:**

- CHIMNEY
- GUTTERS & DOWNSPOUTS
- SOFITS & FASCIA
- YEAR ROOF WAS REPLACED:

GARAGE CONDITION: GOOD OK BAD **NOTES:**

- CEILING
- DOORS
- FLOORS & WALLS
- YEAR DOOR OPENERS WERE REPLACED:

YARD CONDITION: GOOD OK BAD **NOTES:**

- DRAINAGE
- FENCES & GATES
- RETAINING WALL
- SPRINKLER SYSTEM

PROPERTY INSPECTION
Checklist

OTHER IMPORTANT AREAS: GOOD OK BAD **NOTES:**

FOUNDATION

MASONRY VENEERS

EXTERIOR PAINT

STORM WINDOWS

PLUMBING

ELECTRICAL OUTLETS

FLOORING IN ROOMS

WOOD TRIM

FIREPLACE

KITCHEN CONDITION: GOOD OK BAD **NOTES:**

WORKING EXHAUST FAN

NO LEAKS IN PIPES

APPLIANCES OPERATE

OTHER:

BATHROOM CONDITION: GOOD OK BAD **NOTES:**

PROPER DRAINAGE

NO LEAKS IN PIPES

CAULKING IN GOOD SHAPE

TILES ARE SECURE

MISC: GOOD OK BAD **NOTES:**

SMOKE & CARBON DETECTORS

STAIRWAY TREADS SOLID

STAIR HANDRAILS INSTALLED

OTHER:

OTHER:

OTHER:

STICK FLOOR PLAN HERE
(if available)

HOUSE HUNTING *Checklist*

HOUSE SCORE:

PROPERTY ADDRESS

ASKING PRICE:

PROPERTY TAXES:

LOT SIZE:

PROPERTY SIZE:

FINISH: ☐ BRICK ☐ STUCCO ☐ WOOD ☐ SIDING

AGE OF PROPERTY:

NEIGHBORHOOD

DISTANCE TO SCHOOLS:

DISTANCE TO WORK:

PUBLIC TRANSPORTATION:

MEDICAL:

RECREATION:

SHOPPING:

ADDITIONAL INFO:

NOTES:

HOUSE HUNTING

DETAILED HOUSE FEATURES:

OF BEDROOMS: # OF BATHROOMS:

BASEMENT: HEATING TYPE:

PROPERTY CHECKLIST:

POOL	☐	BONUS ROOM	☐
GARAGE	☐	LAUNDRY CHUTE	☐
FIREPLACE	☐	FENCED YARD	☐
EN-SUITE	☐	APPLIANCES	☐
OFFICE	☐	A/C	☐
DECK	☐	HEAT PUMP	☐

NOTES

PARKING ☐
CLOSETS ☐
STORAGE ☐

NOTES

PROPERTY INSPECTION
Checklist

EXTERIOR CONDITION: GOOD   OK   BAD   **NOTES:**

- EXTERIOR OF PROPERTY
- FRONT DOOR
- PORCH/DECK/PATIO
- DRIVEWAY
- GARAGE DOORS
- OUTDOOR LIGHTING
- PAINT & TRIM
- WINDOWS
- WALKWAY

ROOF CONDITION: GOOD   OK   BAD   **NOTES:**

- CHIMNEY
- GUTTERS & DOWNSPOUTS
- SOFITS & FASCIA

YEAR ROOF WAS REPLACED: _____

GARAGE CONDITION: GOOD   OK   BAD   **NOTES:**

- CEILING
- DOORS
- FLOORS & WALLS

YEAR DOOR OPENERS WERE REPLACED: _____

YARD CONDITION: GOOD   OK   BAD   **NOTES:**

- DRAINAGE
- FENCES & GATES
- RETAINING WALL
- SPRINKLER SYSTEM

PROPERTY INSPECTION *Checklist*

OTHER IMPORTANT AREAS: GOOD   OK   BAD   **NOTES:**

FOUNDATION

MASONRY VENEERS

EXTERIOR PAINT

STORM WINDOWS

PLUMBING

ELECTRICAL OUTLETS

FLOORING IN ROOMS

WOOD TRIM

FIREPLACE

KITCHEN CONDITION: GOOD   OK   BAD   **NOTES:**

WORKING EXHAUST FAN

NO LEAKS IN PIPES

APPLIANCES OPERATE

OTHER:

BATHROOM CONDITION: GOOD   OK   BAD   **NOTES:**

PROPER DRAINAGE

NO LEAKS IN PIPES

CAULKING IN GOOD SHAPE

TILES ARE SECURE

MISC: GOOD   OK   BAD   **NOTES:**

SMOKE & CARBON DETECTORS

STAIRWAY TREADS SOLID

STAIR HANDRAILS INSTALLED

OTHER:

OTHER:

OTHER:

STICK FLOOR PLAN HERE
(if available)

HOUSE SCORE:

PROPERTY ADDRESS

ASKING PRICE: PROPERTY TAXES:

LOT SIZE: PROPERTY SIZE:

FINISH: ☐ BRICK ☐ STUCCO ☐ WOOD ☐ SIDING   AGE OF PROPERTY:

NEIGHBORHOOD

DISTANCE TO SCHOOLS: DISTANCE TO WORK:

PUBLIC TRANSPORTATION: MEDICAL:

RECREATION: SHOPPING:

ADDITIONAL INFO: NOTES:

HOUSE HUNTING

DETAILED HOUSE FEATURES:

OF BEDROOMS: # OF BATHROOMS:

BASEMENT: HEATING TYPE:

PROPERTY CHECKLIST:

POOL	☐	BONUS ROOM	☐	NOTES
GARAGE	☐	LAUNDRY CHUTE	☐	
FIREPLACE	☐	FENCED YARD	☐	
EN-SUITE	☐	APPLIANCES	☐	
OFFICE	☐	A/C	☐	
DECK	☐	HEAT PUMP	☐	

PARKING	☐	NOTES
CLOSETS	☐	
STORAGE	☐	

PROPERTY INSPECTION *Checklist*

EXTERIOR CONDITION: GOOD   OK   BAD   **NOTES:**

- EXTERIOR OF PROPERTY
- FRONT DOOR
- PORCH/DECK/PATIO
- DRIVEWAY
- GARAGE DOORS
- OUTDOOR LIGHTING
- PAINT & TRIM
- WINDOWS
- WALKWAY

ROOF CONDITION: GOOD   OK   BAD   **NOTES:**

- CHIMNEY
- GUTTERS & DOWNSPOUTS
- SOFITS & FASCIA

YEAR ROOF WAS REPLACED: _____

GARAGE CONDITION: GOOD   OK   BAD   **NOTES:**

- CEILING
- DOORS
- FLOORS & WALLS

YEAR DOOR OPENERS WERE REPLACED: _____

YARD CONDITION: GOOD   OK   BAD   **NOTES:**

- DRAINAGE
- FENCES & GATES
- RETAINING WALL
- SPRINKLER SYSTEM

PROPERTY INSPECTION
Checklist

OTHER IMPORTANT AREAS: GOOD OK BAD **NOTES:**

FOUNDATION

MASONRY VENEERS

EXTERIOR PAINT

STORM WINDOWS

PLUMBING

ELECTRICAL OUTLETS

FLOORING IN ROOMS

WOOD TRIM

FIREPLACE

KITCHEN CONDITION: GOOD OK BAD **NOTES:**

WORKING EXHAUST FAN

NO LEAKS IN PIPES

APPLIANCES OPERATE

OTHER:

BATHROOM CONDITION: GOOD OK BAD **NOTES:**

PROPER DRAINAGE

NO LEAKS IN PIPES

CAULKING IN GOOD SHAPE

TILES ARE SECURE

MISC: GOOD OK BAD **NOTES:**

SMOKE & CARBON DETECTORS

STAIRWAY TREADS SOLID

STAIR HANDRAILS INSTALLED

OTHER:

OTHER:

OTHER:

STICK FLOOR PLAN HERE
(if available)

HOUSE HUNTING

HOUSE SCORE:

PROPERTY ADDRESS

ASKING PRICE: PROPERTY TAXES:

LOT SIZE: PROPERTY SIZE:

FINISH: ☐ BRICK ☐ STUCCO   AGE OF PROPERTY:
         ☐ WOOD   ☐ SIDING

NEIGHBORHOOD

DISTANCE TO SCHOOLS: DISTANCE TO WORK:

PUBLIC TRANSPORTATION: MEDICAL:

RECREATION: SHOPPING:

ADDITIONAL INFO: NOTES:

HOUSE HUNTING

DETAILED HOUSE FEATURES:

OF BEDROOMS: # OF BATHROOMS:

BASEMENT: HEATING TYPE:

PROPERTY CHECKLIST:

		NOTES
POOL ☐	BONUS ROOM ☐	
GARAGE ☐	LAUNDRY CHUTE ☐	
FIREPLACE ☐	FENCED YARD ☐	
EN-SUITE ☐	APPLIANCES ☐	
OFFICE ☐	A/C ☐	
DECK ☐	HEAT PUMP ☐	

NOTES

- PARKING ☐
- CLOSETS ☐
- STORAGE ☐

PROPERTY INSPECTION *Checklist*

EXTERIOR CONDITION: GOOD   OK   BAD   **NOTES:**

- EXTERIOR OF PROPERTY
- FRONT DOOR
- PORCH/DECK/PATIO
- DRIVEWAY
- GARAGE DOORS
- OUTDOOR LIGHTING
- PAINT & TRIM
- WINDOWS
- WALKWAY

ROOF CONDITION: GOOD   OK   BAD   **NOTES:**

- CHIMNEY
- GUTTERS & DOWNSPOUTS
- SOFITS & FASCIA
- YEAR ROOF WAS REPLACED:

GARAGE CONDITION: GOOD   OK   BAD   **NOTES:**

- CEILING
- DOORS
- FLOORS & WALLS
- YEAR DOOR OPENERS WERE REPLACED:

YARD CONDITION: GOOD   OK   BAD   **NOTES:**

- DRAINAGE
- FENCES & GATES
- RETAINING WALL
- SPRINKLER SYSTEM

PROPERTY INSPECTION *Checklist*

OTHER IMPORTANT AREAS: GOOD   OK   BAD   **NOTES:**

FOUNDATION

MASONRY VENEERS

EXTERIOR PAINT

STORM WINDOWS

PLUMBING

ELECTRICAL OUTLETS

FLOORING IN ROOMS

WOOD TRIM

FIREPLACE

KITCHEN CONDITION: GOOD   OK   BAD   **NOTES:**

WORKING EXHAUST FAN

NO LEAKS IN PIPES

APPLIANCES OPERATE

OTHER:

BATHROOM CONDITION: GOOD   OK   BAD   **NOTES:**

PROPER DRAINAGE

NO LEAKS IN PIPES

CAULKING IN GOOD SHAPE

TILES ARE SECURE

MISC: GOOD   OK   BAD   **NOTES:**

SMOKE & CARBON DETECTORS

STAIRWAY TREADS SOLID

STAIR HANDRAILS INSTALLED

OTHER:

OTHER:

OTHER:

STICK FLOOR PLAN HERE
(if available)

HOUSE SCORE:

PROPERTY ADDRESS

ASKING PRICE: PROPERTY TAXES:

LOT SIZE: PROPERTY SIZE:

FINISH: ☐ BRICK   ☐ STUCCO   AGE OF PROPERTY:
          ☐ WOOD   ☐ SIDING

NEIGHBORHOOD

DISTANCE TO SCHOOLS: DISTANCE TO WORK:

PUBLIC TRANSPORTATION: MEDICAL:

RECREATION: SHOPPING:

ADDITIONAL INFO: NOTES:

HOUSE HUNTING

DETAILED HOUSE FEATURES:

OF BEDROOMS: # OF BATHROOMS:

BASEMENT: HEATING TYPE:

PROPERTY CHECKLIST:

POOL	☐	BONUS ROOM	☐	NOTES
GARAGE	☐	LAUNDRY CHUTE	☐	
FIREPLACE	☐	FENCED YARD	☐	
EN-SUITE	☐	APPLIANCES	☐	
OFFICE	☐	A/C	☐	
DECK	☐	HEAT PUMP	☐	

PARKING	☐	NOTES
CLOSETS	☐	
STORAGE	☐	

PROPERTY INSPECTION
Checklist

EXTERIOR CONDITION: GOOD   OK   BAD   **NOTES:**

- EXTERIOR OF PROPERTY
- FRONT DOOR
- PORCH/DECK/PATIO
- DRIVEWAY
- GARAGE DOORS
- OUTDOOR LIGHTING
- PAINT & TRIM
- WINDOWS
- WALKWAY

ROOF CONDITION: GOOD   OK   BAD   **NOTES:**

- CHIMNEY
- GUTTERS & DOWNSPOUTS
- SOFITS & FASCIA
- YEAR ROOF WAS REPLACED: _____

GARAGE CONDITION: GOOD   OK   BAD   **NOTES:**

- CEILING
- DOORS
- FLOORS & WALLS
- YEAR DOOR OPENERS WERE REPLACED: _____

YARD CONDITION: GOOD   OK   BAD   **NOTES:**

- DRAINAGE
- FENCES & GATES
- RETAINING WALL
- SPRINKLER SYSTEM

PROPERTY INSPECTION
Checklist

OTHER IMPORTANT AREAS: GOOD OK BAD   **NOTES:**

- FOUNDATION
- MASONRY VENEERS
- EXTERIOR PAINT
- STORM WINDOWS
- PLUMBING
- ELECTRICAL OUTLETS
- FLOORING IN ROOMS
- WOOD TRIM
- FIREPLACE

KITCHEN CONDITION: GOOD OK BAD   **NOTES:**

- WORKING EXHAUST FAN
- NO LEAKS IN PIPES
- APPLIANCES OPERATE
- OTHER:

BATHROOM CONDITION: GOOD OK BAD   **NOTES:**

- PROPER DRAINAGE
- NO LEAKS IN PIPES
- CAULKING IN GOOD SHAPE
- TILES ARE SECURE

MISC: GOOD OK BAD   **NOTES:**

- SMOKE & CARBON DETECTORS
- STAIRWAY TREADS SOLID
- STAIR HANDRAILS INSTALLED
- OTHER:
- OTHER:
- OTHER:

STICK FLOOR PLAN HERE
(if available)

HOUSE HUNTING *Checklist*

HOUSE SCORE:

PROPERTY ADDRESS

ASKING PRICE: PROPERTY TAXES:

LOT SIZE: PROPERTY SIZE:

FINISH: ☐ BRICK ☐ STUCCO   AGE OF PROPERTY:
         ☐ WOOD   ☐ SIDING

NEIGHBORHOOD

DISTANCE TO SCHOOLS: DISTANCE TO WORK:

PUBLIC TRANSPORTATION: MEDICAL:

RECREATION: SHOPPING:

ADDITIONAL INFO: NOTES:

HOUSE HUNTING

DETAILED HOUSE FEATURES:

OF BEDROOMS: # OF BATHROOMS:

BASEMENT: HEATING TYPE:

PROPERTY CHECKLIST:

POOL	☐	BONUS ROOM	☐	NOTES
GARAGE	☐	LAUNDRY CHUTE	☐	
FIREPLACE	☐	FENCED YARD	☐	
EN-SUITE	☐	APPLIANCES	☐	
OFFICE	☐	A/C	☐	
DECK	☐	HEAT PUMP	☐	

PARKING	☐	NOTES
CLOSETS	☐	
STORAGE	☐	

PROPERTY INSPECTION *Checklist*

EXTERIOR CONDITION: GOOD OK BAD **NOTES:**

- EXTERIOR OF PROPERTY
- FRONT DOOR
- PORCH/DECK/PATIO
- DRIVEWAY
- GARAGE DOORS
- OUTDOOR LIGHTING
- PAINT & TRIM
- WINDOWS
- WALKWAY

ROOF CONDITION: GOOD OK BAD **NOTES:**

- CHIMNEY
- GUTTERS & DOWNSPOUTS
- SOFITS & FASCIA
- YEAR ROOF WAS REPLACED: _____

GARAGE CONDITION: GOOD OK BAD **NOTES:**

- CEILING
- DOORS
- FLOORS & WALLS
- YEAR DOOR OPENERS WERE REPLACED: _____

YARD CONDITION: GOOD OK BAD **NOTES:**

- DRAINAGE
- FENCES & GATES
- RETAINING WALL
- SPRINKLER SYSTEM

PROPERTY INSPECTION *Checklist*

OTHER IMPORTANT AREAS: GOOD OK BAD **NOTES:**

FOUNDATION

MASONRY VENEERS

EXTERIOR PAINT

STORM WINDOWS

PLUMBING

ELECTRICAL OUTLETS

FLOORING IN ROOMS

WOOD TRIM

FIREPLACE

KITCHEN CONDITION: GOOD OK BAD **NOTES:**

WORKING EXHAUST FAN

NO LEAKS IN PIPES

APPLIANCES OPERATE

OTHER:

BATHROOM CONDITION: GOOD OK BAD **NOTES:**

PROPER DRAINAGE

NO LEAKS IN PIPES

CAULKING IN GOOD SHAPE

TILES ARE SECURE

MISC: GOOD OK BAD **NOTES:**

SMOKE & CARBON DETECTORS

STAIRWAY TREADS SOLID

STAIR HANDRAILS INSTALLED

OTHER:

OTHER:

OTHER:

STICK FLOOR PLAN HERE
(if available)

House Hunting NOTES

House Hunting NOTES

House Hunting NOTES

House Hunting NOTES

House Hunting NOTES

House Hunting NOTES

House Hunting NOTES

THE BIG
move

Congratulations!

You bought a house!

Now it's time to prepare for the move to make the process as smooth and stress free as possible.

TO DO: *Current Residence*

DATE:

MOST IMPORTANT

NOTES:

TO DO: *New Residence*

DATE: **MOST IMPORTANT**

NOTES:

MOVING DAY *Planner*

6-WEEKS PRIOR

- HIRE A MOVING COMPANY
- KEEP RECEIPTS FOR TAX PURPOSES
- DETERMINE A BUDGET FOR MOVING EXPENSES
- ORGANIZE INVENTORY
- GET PACKING BOXES & LABELS
- PURGE / GIVE AWAY / SELL UNWANTED ITEMS
- CREATE AN INVENTORY SHEET OF ITEMS & BOXES
- RESEARCH SCHOOLS FOR YOUR CHILDREN
- PLAN A GARAGE SALE TO UNLOAD UNWANTED ITEMS

4-WEEKS PRIOR

- CONFIRM DATES WITH MOVING COMPANY
- RESEARCH YOUR NEW COMMUNITY
- START PACKING BOXES
- PURCHASE MOVING INSURANCE
- ORGANIZE FINANCIAL & LEGAL DOCUMENTS IN ONE PLACE
- FIND SNOW REMOVAL OR LANDSCAPE SERVICE FOR NEW RESIDENCE
- RESEARCH NEW DOCTOR, DENTIST, VETERNARIAN, ETC

2-WEEKS PRIOR

- PLAN FOR PET TRANSPORT DURING MOVE
- SET UP MAIL FORWARDING SERVICE
- TRANSFER HOMEOWNERS INSURANCE TO NEW RESIDENCE
- TRANSFER UTILITIES TO NEW RESIDENCE
- UPDATE YOUR DRIVER'S LICENSE

MOVING DAY *Planner*

6-WEEKS PRIOR

4-WEEKS PRIOR

2-WEEKS PRIOR

MOVING DAY *Planner*

WEEK OF MOVE

MOVING DAY

NOTES & REMINDERS

MOVING DAY *Planner*

PRIORITIES

MOVING DAY SCHEDULE

6 AM
7 AM
8 AM
9 AM
10 AM
11 AM
12 PM
1 PM
2 PM
3 PM
4 PM
5 PM
6 PM
7 PM
8 PM
9 PM
10 PM
11 PM
12 AM

MOVING DAY TO DO LIST

ORGANIZATION

REMINDERS

MOVING DAY *List*

OLD RESIDENCE

NEW RESIDENCE

MOVING DAY List

OLD RESIDENCE

NEW RESIDENCE

Moving NOTES

Moving NOTES

ADDRESS CHANGE
Checklist

UTILITIES:

- ELECTRIC
- CABLE/SATELLITE
- GAS
- SECURITY SYSTEM
- PHONE
- INTERNET
- WATER/SEWER
- OTHER
- OTHER
- OTHER

FINANCIAL:

- BANK
- CREDIT CARD
- BANK STATEMENTS
- EMPLOYER
- INSURANCE
- OTHER
- OTHER
- OTHER
- OTHER
- OTHER

START/STOP *Utilities*

ELECTRIC COMPANY

NAME

PHONE

WEBSITE URL

START DATE

STOP DATE

ACCOUNT NUMBER

INTERNET SERVICE PROVIDER

NAME

PHONE

WEBSITE URL

START DATE

STOP DATE

ACCOUNT NUMBER

GAS / HEATING COMPANY

NAME

PHONE

WEBSITE URL

START DATE

STOP DATE

ACCOUNT NUMBER

START/STOP *Utilities*

CABLE/SATELLITE

NAME

PHONE

WEBSITE URL

START DATE

STOP DATE

ACCOUNT NUMBER

SECURITY SYSTEM

NAME

PHONE

WEBSITE URL

START DATE

STOP DATE

ACCOUNT NUMBER

OTHER:

NAME

PHONE

WEBSITE URL

START DATE

STOP DATE

ACCOUNT NUMBER

NOTES:

NEW PROVIDER *Contacts*

MEDICAL

FAMILY DOCTOR

NAME:

PHONE:

EMAIL:

ADDRESS:

WEBSITE URL:

PEDIATRICIAN

NAME:

PHONE:

EMAIL:

ADDRESS:

WEBSITE URL:

VET

NAME:

PHONE:

EMAIL:

ADDRESS:

WEBSITE URL:

NOTES

NEW PROVIDER *Contacts*

EDUCATION

SCHOOL #1:

NAME:

PHONE:

EMAIL:

ADDRESS:

WEBSITE URL:

SCHOOL #2:

NAME:

PHONE:

EMAIL:

ADDRESS:

WEBSITE URL:

SCHOOL #3:

NAME:

PHONE:

EMAIL:

ADDRESS:

WEBSITE URL:

NOTES

IMPORTANT *Dates*

MONTH:

NOTES & REMINDERS

Packing NOTES

Packing NOTES

Packing NOTES

MOVING BOX *Inventory*

ROOM: BOX NO: COLOR CODE:

CONTENTS:

ROOM: BOX NO: COLOR CODE:

CONTENTS:

ROOM: BOX NO: COLOR CODE:

CONTENTS:

ROOM: BOX NO: COLOR CODE:

CONTENTS:

MOVING BOX *Inventory*

ROOM: BOX NO: COLOR CODE:

CONTENTS:

ROOM: BOX NO: COLOR CODE:

CONTENTS:

ROOM: BOX NO: COLOR CODE:

CONTENTS:

ROOM: BOX NO: COLOR CODE:

CONTENTS:

MOVING BOX *Inventory*

ROOM: BOX NO: COLOR CODE:

CONTENTS:

ROOM: BOX NO: COLOR CODE:

CONTENTS:

ROOM: BOX NO: COLOR CODE:

CONTENTS:

ROOM: BOX NO: COLOR CODE:

CONTENTS:

MOVING BOX *Inventory*

ROOM: BOX NO: COLOR CODE:

CONTENTS:

ROOM: BOX NO: COLOR CODE:

CONTENTS:

ROOM: BOX NO: COLOR CODE:

CONTENTS:

ROOM: BOX NO: COLOR CODE:

CONTENTS:

MOVING BOX *Inventory*

ROOM: **BOX NO:**   **COLOR CODE:**

CONTENTS:

ROOM: **BOX NO:**   **COLOR CODE:**

CONTENTS:

ROOM: **BOX NO:**   **COLOR CODE:**

CONTENTS:

ROOM: **BOX NO:**   **COLOR CODE:**

CONTENTS:

MOVING BOX *Inventory*

ROOM: **BOX NO:** **COLOR CODE:**

CONTENTS:

ROOM: **BOX NO:** **COLOR CODE:**

CONTENTS:

ROOM: **BOX NO:** **COLOR CODE:**

CONTENTS:

ROOM: **BOX NO:** **COLOR CODE:**

CONTENTS:

MOVING BOX *Inventory*

ROOM: **BOX NO:**   **COLOR CODE:**

CONTENTS:

ROOM: **BOX NO:**   **COLOR CODE:**

CONTENTS:

ROOM: **BOX NO:**   **COLOR CODE:**

CONTENTS:

ROOM: **BOX NO:**   **COLOR CODE:**

CONTENTS:

MOVING BOX *Inventory*

ROOM:	BOX NO:	COLOR CODE:

CONTENTS:

ROOM:	BOX NO:	COLOR CODE:

CONTENTS:

ROOM:	BOX NO:	COLOR CODE:

CONTENTS:

ROOM:	BOX NO:	COLOR CODE:

CONTENTS:

MOVING BOX *Inventory*

ROOM: BOX NO: COLOR CODE:

CONTENTS:

ROOM: BOX NO: COLOR CODE:

CONTENTS:

ROOM: BOX NO: COLOR CODE:

CONTENTS:

ROOM: BOX NO: COLOR CODE:

CONTENTS:

MOVING BOX *Inventory*

ROOM: **BOX NO:**   **COLOR CODE:**

CONTENTS:

ROOM: **BOX NO:**   **COLOR CODE:**

CONTENTS:

ROOM: **BOX NO:**   **COLOR CODE:**

CONTENTS:

ROOM: **BOX NO:**   **COLOR CODE:**

CONTENTS:

MOVING BOX *Inventory*

ROOM: BOX NO: COLOR CODE:

CONTENTS:

ROOM: BOX NO: COLOR CODE:

CONTENTS:

ROOM: BOX NO: COLOR CODE:

CONTENTS:

ROOM: BOX NO: COLOR CODE:

CONTENTS:

MOVING BOX *Inventory*

ROOM: **BOX NO:**   **COLOR CODE:**

CONTENTS:

ROOM: **BOX NO:**   **COLOR CODE:**

CONTENTS:

ROOM: **BOX NO:**   **COLOR CODE:**

CONTENTS:

ROOM: **BOX NO:**   **COLOR CODE:**

CONTENTS:

MOVING BOX *Inventory*

ROOM: **BOX NO:**   **COLOR CODE:**

CONTENTS:

ROOM: **BOX NO:**   **COLOR CODE:**

CONTENTS:

ROOM: **BOX NO:**   **COLOR CODE:**

CONTENTS:

ROOM: **BOX NO:**   **COLOR CODE:**

CONTENTS:

MOVING BOX *Inventory*

ROOM:　　　　　　　BOX NO:　　　　　　　COLOR CODE:

CONTENTS:

ROOM:　　　　　　　BOX NO:　　　　　　　COLOR CODE:

CONTENTS:

ROOM:　　　　　　　BOX NO:　　　　　　　COLOR CODE:

CONTENTS:

ROOM:　　　　　　　BOX NO:　　　　　　　COLOR CODE:

CONTENTS:

MOVING BOX *Inventory*

ROOM: BOX NO: COLOR CODE:

CONTENTS:

ROOM: BOX NO: COLOR CODE:

CONTENTS:

ROOM: BOX NO: COLOR CODE:

CONTENTS:

ROOM: BOX NO: COLOR CODE:

CONTENTS:

MOVING BOX *Inventory*

ROOM:	BOX NO:	COLOR CODE:

CONTENTS:

ROOM:	BOX NO:	COLOR CODE:

CONTENTS:

ROOM:	BOX NO:	COLOR CODE:

CONTENTS:

ROOM:	BOX NO:	COLOR CODE:

CONTENTS:

MOVING BOX *Inventory*

ROOM: **BOX NO:**   **COLOR CODE:**

CONTENTS:

ROOM: **BOX NO:**   **COLOR CODE:**

CONTENTS:

ROOM: **BOX NO:**   **COLOR CODE:**

CONTENTS:

ROOM: **BOX NO:**   **COLOR CODE:**

CONTENTS:

MOVING BOX *Inventory*

ROOM: BOX NO: COLOR CODE:

CONTENTS:

ROOM: BOX NO: COLOR CODE:

CONTENTS:

ROOM: BOX NO: COLOR CODE:

CONTENTS:

ROOM: BOX NO: COLOR CODE:

CONTENTS:

MOVING BOX *Inventory*

ROOM: BOX NO: COLOR CODE:

CONTENTS:

ROOM: BOX NO: COLOR CODE:

CONTENTS:

ROOM: BOX NO: COLOR CODE:

CONTENTS:

ROOM: BOX NO: COLOR CODE:

CONTENTS:

MOVING BOX *Inventory*

ROOM: **BOX NO:**   **COLOR CODE:**

CONTENTS:

ROOM: **BOX NO:**   **COLOR CODE:**

CONTENTS:

ROOM: **BOX NO:**   **COLOR CODE:**

CONTENTS:

ROOM: **BOX NO:**   **COLOR CODE:**

CONTENTS:

MOVING BOX *Inventory*

ROOM: BOX NO: COLOR CODE:

CONTENTS:

ROOM: BOX NO: COLOR CODE:

CONTENTS:

ROOM: BOX NO: COLOR CODE:

CONTENTS:

ROOM: BOX NO: COLOR CODE:

CONTENTS:

MOVING BOX *Inventory*

ROOM:　　　　　BOX NO:　　　　　COLOR CODE:

CONTENTS:

ROOM:　　　　　BOX NO:　　　　　COLOR CODE:

CONTENTS:

ROOM:　　　　　BOX NO:　　　　　COLOR CODE:

CONTENTS:

ROOM:　　　　　BOX NO:　　　　　COLOR CODE:

CONTENTS:

MOVING BOX *Inventory*

ROOM: BOX NO: COLOR CODE:

CONTENTS:

ROOM: BOX NO: COLOR CODE:

CONTENTS:

ROOM: BOX NO: COLOR CODE:

CONTENTS:

ROOM: BOX NO: COLOR CODE:

CONTENTS:

MOVING BOX *Inventory*

ROOM:　　　　　　　BOX NO:　　　　　　　COLOR CODE:

CONTENTS:

ROOM:　　　　　　　BOX NO:　　　　　　　COLOR CODE:

CONTENTS:

ROOM:　　　　　　　BOX NO:　　　　　　　COLOR CODE:

CONTENTS:

ROOM:　　　　　　　BOX NO:　　　　　　　COLOR CODE:

CONTENTS:

MOVING BOX *Inventory*

ROOM: BOX NO: COLOR CODE:

CONTENTS:

ROOM: BOX NO: COLOR CODE:

CONTENTS:

ROOM: BOX NO: COLOR CODE:

CONTENTS:

ROOM: BOX NO: COLOR CODE:

CONTENTS:

ROOM *Planner*

ROOM:

PAINT COLORS::

COLOR SCHEME:

DÉCOR IDEAS:

FURNITURE IDEAS:

NOTES:

ROOM:

PAINT COLORS::

COLOR SCHEME:

DÉCOR IDEAS:

FURNITURE IDEAS:

NOTES:

NEW ROOM *Planner*

ROOM:

PAINT COLORS::

COLOR CODE:

DÉCOR IDEAS:

FURNITURE IDEAS:

THINGS TO DO:

- [ ]
- [ ]
- [ ]
- [ ]
- [ ]
- [ ]
- [ ]
- [ ]
- [ ]
- [ ]
- [ ]
- [ ]

DÉCOR IDEAS:

NEW ROOM *Planner*

ROOM:

PAINT COLORS::

COLOR CODE:

DÉCOR IDEAS:

FURNITURE IDEAS:

THINGS TO DO:

☐
☐
☐
☐
☐
☐
☐
☐
☐
☐
☐
☐

DÉCOR IDEAS:

NEW ROOM *Planner*

ROOM:

PAINT COLORS::

COLOR CODE:

DÉCOR IDEAS:

FURNITURE IDEAS:

THINGS TO DO:

- [ ]
- [ ]
- [ ]
- [ ]
- [ ]
- [ ]
- [ ]
- [ ]
- [ ]
- [ ]
- [ ]
- [ ]

DÉCOR IDEAS:

NEW ROOM *Planner*

ROOM:

PAINT COLORS::

COLOR CODE:

DÉCOR IDEAS:

FURNITURE IDEAS:

THINGS TO DO:

☐
☐
☐
☐
☐
☐
☐
☐
☐
☐
☐

DÉCOR IDEAS:

NEW ROOM *Planner*

ROOM:

PAINT COLORS::

COLOR CODE:

DÉCOR IDEAS:

FURNITURE IDEAS:

THINGS TO DO:

- [ ]
- [ ]
- [ ]
- [ ]
- [ ]
- [ ]
- [ ]
- [ ]
- [ ]
- [ ]
- [ ]
- [ ]

DÉCOR IDEAS:

NEW ROOM *Planner*

ROOM:

PAINT COLORS::

COLOR CODE:

DÉCOR IDEAS:

FURNITURE IDEAS:

THINGS TO DO:

☐
☐
☐
☐
☐
☐
☐
☐
☐
☐
☐

DÉCOR IDEAS:

NEW ROOM *Planner*

ROOM:

PAINT COLORS::

COLOR CODE:

DÉCOR IDEAS:

FURNITURE IDEAS:

THINGS TO DO:

- [ ]
- [ ]
- [ ]
- [ ]
- [ ]
- [ ]
- [ ]
- [ ]
- [ ]
- [ ]
- [ ]

DÉCOR IDEAS:

NEW ROOM *Planner*

ROOM:

PAINT COLORS::

COLOR CODE:

DÉCOR IDEAS:

FURNITURE IDEAS:

THINGS TO DO:

- [ ]
- [ ]
- [ ]
- [ ]
- [ ]
- [ ]
- [ ]
- [ ]
- [ ]
- [ ]
- [ ]

DÉCOR IDEAS:

NEW ROOM *Planner*

ROOM:

PAINT COLORS::

COLOR CODE:

DÉCOR IDEAS:

FURNITURE IDEAS:

THINGS TO DO:

- [ ]
- [ ]
- [ ]
- [ ]
- [ ]
- [ ]
- [ ]
- [ ]
- [ ]
- [ ]
- [ ]

DÉCOR IDEAS:

NEW ROOM *Planner*

ROOM:

PAINT COLORS::

COLOR CODE:

DÉCOR IDEAS:

FURNITURE IDEAS:

THINGS TO DO:

- [ ]
- [ ]
- [ ]
- [ ]
- [ ]
- [ ]
- [ ]
- [ ]
- [ ]
- [ ]
- [ ]

DÉCOR IDEAS:

NEW ROOM *Planner*

ROOM:

PAINT COLORS::

COLOR CODE:

DÉCOR IDEAS:

FURNITURE IDEAS:

THINGS TO DO:

☐
☐
☐
☐
☐
☐
☐
☐
☐
☐
☐

DÉCOR IDEAS:

My Personal NOTES

My Personal NOTES

My Personal NOTES

My Personal NOTES

My Personal NOTES

My Personal NOTES

Made in the USA
Monee, IL
11 December 2020